To a Wonderful Daughter
With Love

To a Wonderful Daughter With Love

Selected by
Kitty McDonald Clevenger

Hallmark Editions

The publisher wishes to thank those who have given their kind permission to reprint
material included in this book. Every effort has been made to give proper
acknowledgments. Any omissions or errors are deeply regretted, and the publisher,
upon notification, will be pleased to make necessary corrections in subsequent
editions.

ACKNOWLEDGMENTS: "A Daughter's Glory" from To My Daughters With Love by
Pearl Buck. Copyright 1949, © 1957, 1960, 1962, 1963, 1964 by Pearl S. Buck.
Copyright © 1967 by The Pearl S. Buck Foundation, Inc. Reprinted by permission of
Thomas Y. Crowell Company, Inc. and Harold Ober Associates Incorporated. "Going
Forth" by Margaret Mead from Family. Copyright 1966 by Margaret Mead and Ken
Heyman. Reprinted with permission. "To My Daughter" by Stephen Spender.
Copyright © 1955 by Stephen Spender. Reprinted from Selected Poems, by Stephen
Spender, by permission of Random House, Inc. and Faber and Faber Limited. "Small
Girls" by Ruth Ehrlen Goodman from the January 1975 issue of Good
Housekeeping. © 1975 by the Hearst Corporation. Reprinted with permission.
"Two" by Maureen Cannon from Ladies' Home Journal. © 1971 by Maureen Cannon.
Reprinted with permission. "To a Daughter, Growing" by Maureen Cannon from the
August 1975 issue of Good Housekeeping. © 1975 by Maureen Cannon. Reprinted
with permission. "Prayer for a Daughter" from The Wind Carved Tree by Esther Wood.
Copyright 1953 by Esther Wood. Reprinted with permission.

To a Wonderful Daughter
With Love

A Daughter's Gifts

A daughter brings sunshine
    to brighten your days
With a magic that's found
    in her warm, loving ways.
A daughter brings beauty
    and grace to a home
With a wonderful charm
    that is hers all alone.

Her smile has the magic
    of flowers in bloom.
Her laughter brings gladness
    and warmth to a room.
The sweet things she's done
    and the nice things she's said
Are memories to cherish
    throughout years ahead!

Alan Doan

A Small Daughter Walking Outdoors

Easy, wind!
Go softly here!
She is small
And very dear.

She is young
And cannot say
Words to chase
The wind away.

She is new
To walking, so
Wind, be kind
And gently blow

On her ruffled head,
On grass and clover.
Easy, wind …
She'll tumble over!

Frances Frost

They are angels of God in disguise;
    His sunlight still gleams in their tresses;
His glory still gleams in their eyes.

Charles M. Dickinson

6

Age Seven

Second grade. She keeps her counsel
    (Sevens are inclined to do so),
But she dotes on her discoveries
    With the fervor of a Crusoe!
What a wondrous world she lives in,
    All those doorways opening, leading
To a thousand facts and figures...
    Writing, spelling, science, reading!

Wait, though, what can slow her whizzing
    To a walk? Aghast, she lingers
In arithmetic's abyss when,
    Weeping, she "runs out of fingers"!

Kathleen Halliday

Touched by her special magic,
the world comes alive once more…
but brighter and more beautiful than ever before.
Old dreams are rekindled…
lost visions returned…
Life shines with new wonder,
and each day, each hour holds a fresh surprise
when seen through a daughter's sparkling eyes.

Elizabeth Plowman

A daughter is a beauty
Whose heart is filled with spring,
And her gentleness is but a part
Of all the joy her graces bring.

Charlotte Carpenter

Two

I have a daughter made of silk
And gossamer and such.
Her sister is a muslin child,
As sturdy to the touch
As homespun is, as warm, as dear.
Beloved both, this much
They've taught me, silken butterfly
And merry muslin moth:
That silk and muslin, woven tightly,
Make a lovely cloth!

Maureen Cannon

Going Forth

For the child must go forth from the warmth
and safety of its mother's care — first to take
a few steps across the room, then to join
playmates, and later to go to school, to work,
to experience courtship and marriage, and to
establish a new home. A girl must learn, as
she walks beside her mother, that she is both
like her mother and a person in her own right.

Margaret Mead

*M*emories of a daughter's precious love
sparkle and shimmer on the stream of time,
each reflecting its own moment of beauty,
its own vision of delight.

Mary Ann Riley

To My Daughter, Newborn

What took you so long, girl? You came
   The roundabout road surely.
I know, you stopped along the way
   To primp, my lass. It's purely
A female trick to tantalize.
   No doubt you tossed your tresses
And shrugged, you sassy miss, and winked.
   I'm winking back. My guess is
You'd other things to do than check
   Your watch. The hands were racing,
But you had dandelions to pick,
   And butterflies for chasing.

No matter, here you are, come in!
   I tease, my way of stating
A joy too deep for words. You've come,
   And, oh, how we've been waiting!

Anne Dexter

Speaking of Little Girls...

A little girl is a gift from heaven, although she only wears her halo on special occasions — and rarely for longer than half an hour. The rest of the time she's too busy climbing, bouncing, dancing, swinging, coloring, getting into and out of mischief and just being her own dear, irritating, lovable, purely original self.

Her moods are as unpredictable as tomorrow's weather and a lot more variable. But she's not much good at keeping secrets; so you're hardly ever in doubt as to how she's feeling at any given moment. It's a proven fact that no creature on earth can cry louder or giggle longer than a little girl.

A little girl much prefers mud puddles to bathtubs, monster cartoons to cultural events and junk food to haute cuisine. She's almost always ready for more dessert, almost never ready for bed.

A little girl is an all-day variety show of jokes, riddles, songs and somersaults, which she generally refuses to perform for company. Though you may not always be up for her routines, you're clearly her favorite audience — and ready or not, here she comes!

With a single frown a little girl can make you feel like a miser, a clown, a heartless traitor or an unspeakable ogre. With a single smile she can convince you that you're the luckiest person alive. Just when you're starting to feel in control of the relationship, she invites you into a delightful world of make-believe, where you are magically transformed from parent to playmate in the twinkling of an eye.

A little girl is a cookie jar filled with love, laughter, surprises and memories that grow sweeter through the years. Every cuddle, every kiss, every heart-to-heart moment she shares will make you feel more blessed and more thankful that she is yours — or rather, that you are hers!

Edward Cunningham

To a Daughter, Growing

Skinny girl, as plain as twelve can be,
Unformed, unfinished, why is there in me
This need to badger time, this urgency
To make the vision flesh-and-blood, to see
The woman grown, complete, inevitably
The "Yes, she will be lovely!" final you
That signs, bewildering now, are pointing to?

Maureen Cannon

Behold the Woman

The land of make-believe is gone;
The dolls with which she used to play
Are sleeping high on closet shelves,
For thus was childhood laid away.
But time transforms a little girl
By adding beauty, charm and grace,
And gives to her that special role
To make the world a better place.
Now proudly dressed in cap and gown
She clasps that all-important scroll.
Her smiling eyes express the thanks
For this — her long-awaited goal.
May hope be always in her heart
And all her happy dreams come true;
Her zeal in serving others keep
The joy of living shining through.
We pray that life will treat her well
And keep her helpful, kind and good,
That she may justly claim the right
To wear the crown of womanhood!

Reginald Holmes

To My Daughter

Bright clasp of her whole hand around my finger,
My daughter, as we walk together now,
All my life I'll feel a ring invisibly
Circle this bone with shining: when she is grown
Far from today as her eyes are far already.

Stephen Spender

Daughters add ribbons and roses to everyday bouquets.

Marjorie Frances Ames

Prayer for a Daughter

God of men and God of nature,
Shape my daughter like the seasons.
Give her all the song of springtime
And the subtlety of April,
Generosity of summer,
Warmth and all the sweet fulfillment,
And the sparkling wit of autumn,
Color like October hillsides.
Lest her charms may be too many,
Give her something of the winter:
Stars and distances and silence,
Courage of the open spaces,
Wisdom of the waiting branches.
Don't forget to give her winter.

Esther Wood

There is a secret magic known only to
daughters. For none but they can keep our
spirits so warm, our hearts so young, our
lives so full of wonder and delight.

Rebecca Shaw

She grows up much too fast…
leaves legacies of pigtails,
freckles, dollies…
becomes a woman all too soon:
but she will always be
her parents' "little girl."

Maria Angilica

Gold

A little girl —
Sometimes she'll bring you
   shoes that need tying,
   tears that need drying.
Sometimes she'll bring you
   toys that need mending,
   hurts that need tending.
Sometimes she'll bring you
   small hands to hold.
But she'll always bring love
   that's more precious than gold.

Amy Cassidy

Joy

Life is filled with wonder day and night—
    Bright new rainbows after morning showers,
Flowers polka-dotting April hills,
    Whippoorwills in tune to welcome spring—
But none can match the joy
    that daughters bring!

J. L. Alderman

Todays are so much sweeter,
    happier and more beautiful
because of all the yesterdays
    a daughter has filled
    with love.

Mary Alice Loberg

$\mathcal{M}$agically, a little storybook princess
blossoms into a proud and lovely woman,
leaving a treasure of beautiful memories for
each year along the way.

Mary Catherine Shannon

*How the world is warmed, brightened,
blessed by a daughter's love!*

Nora M. Kelly

A Daughter

A daughter is sweetness
   with gay, laughing eyes,
Hair ribbons, pinafores, lace,
   A lovable lady
   of charm and delight
With dirt on her dignified face,
   A daughter in no time
     is suddenly grown…

…With a womanly air
   and a mind of her own,
A daughter is pleasure…
   a treasure to those
Who watch with such pride
   as their "little girl" grows.

Susan W. Lee

Small Girls

Small girls,
Like words,
Can enter hearts
Quietly like the
Sound of pen on paper.

Writing their messages
Of happiness
In vast empty
Spaces.

Messages, speaking in
Softness of sweets and
Sounds of tastes moving
As honey from the spoon.

Small girls,
Like words,
Sweetly move us too.

Ruth Ehrlen Goodman

Flowers and Daughters

Daughters and flowers have a lot in common. When a daughter is very young she is a wild thing like the dandelions she brings home to mother in a bedraggled bouquet. But soon a daughter takes on a more regal bearing and her life begins to bloom like a rose. And when she becomes a woman grown, married with children of her own, then she is a perfect thing, pure, full of grace, like a lily. But a daughter still finds joy in the sight of a little dandelion growing up beside her.

Sarah Aldo Benson

Carousels

Little girls on carousels
Have no time for wishing wells
Or secrets that the daisy tells —
There's playing to be done!
With laughing eyes and tossing curls,
Around they go in graceful whirls,
For carousels bring little girls
A magic world of fun!

Mary Catherine Shannon

Daughters may not be angels,
but no one could ever bring
more heaven into our lives.

George Webster Douglas

The presence of a young girl is like the presence of a flower; the one gives its perfume to all that approach it, the other her grace to all that surrounds her.

Louis Desnoyers

$\mathcal{D}$aughters are as different from one another
as are the gardens of springtime. Each
deserves full measures of patience, love and
care. For each holds a promise of special
beauty, of incomparable glory in seasons yet
to come.

George S. Harano

*Surely there is no warmer moment in life
than one spent basking in the sunlight
of a daughter's smile.*

Timothy Carrol

A Daughter's Glory

Accept your womanhood, my daughter, and rejoice in it. It is your glory that you are a woman, for this is why he loves you, he whom you love. Be gentle, be wise, as a woman is gentle and wise. Be ardent and love with a woman's ardor. Through your love, teach him what it means to be a man, a noble man, a strong man. Believe in him, for only through your belief can he believe in himself.

In our secret hearts, man and woman, we long above all else to know that the other, the one we love, knows what we are and believes in what we can be. Is this not romance? Yes, and the highest romance, investing the smallest detail of life with the color of joy.

Pearl Buck

If there is one pure pleasure in life, it is watching a young daughter at play. Running, laughing, dancing, singing — she is as fresh as her bright, new imagination, as vibrant as life itself. And all of springtime blossoms in her smile.

Thomas Gerard Hughes

*Just as the moon is the light of the night
and the sun of the day,
so are good children
the light of their family.*

Mary Dawson Hughes

A Radiance of Daughters

The discovery of language is one of a child's greatest experiences, perhaps more so for a daughter than for a son. A boy is much more likely to *act* in a situation, while a girl in the same scene would more likely speak, especially if it is an event to which the young male would respond with violence.

This same relationship between language and a daughter has affected many writers. When they have written about the little girls inhabiting their house (no, not inhabiting, but giving a radiance to the house), even their prose style has become livelier.

Having written an entire volume of sonnets about my two daughters, I know intensely the love of a daughter for language, and the response that it in turn brings out in a writer-father. In her poem "Prayer for a Daughter," Esther Wood ends with a line any writer would honor: "Don't forget to give her winter." That is to say, be sure she knows the darkness and bitter cold of life as well as its warmth and sweetness.

Say the word "daughter," slowly, prolong its gentle sound. Notice the way it lingers on the tongue like a piece of candy. Then speak the word "son." Doesn't it have, like the masculine creature it names, a greater hardness? Doesn't it disappear from the mouth in the moment of its uttering? In such a difference of simple nouns there is contained the quality of actual difference between the girl and the boy. That distinction carries over into writing about children too....

A good daughter is like a good piece of writing: candid, lyrical, graceful, moving, alive. I have seen a young girl walk across a room, intent on her intense errand, and it was like seeing a voice become visible, as if not her tongue but her motion said, "I will do this for my life."

Paul Engle

Occupied With Dreams

A moment comes in girlhood when the eyes are less occupied with the practical realities about them, than with dreams and visions of enchantment. The young girl has her reserves and her innate reticence, and often her nearest and dearest do not so much as lift a tiny edge of the curtain that drops between her and them. They speak of realities, prosaic affairs of the marketplace and of the present, while for her the true realities wear opal tints and are wreathed in violet mists. She is like the child who looks from the farmhouse door at the range of hills that rims the landscape, wondering what may lie on the other side.

Margaret Sangster

Pattern

Dressed up in her mother's clothes,
Powder smeared upon her nose,
Rubber bands to hold her hose,
She's all grown up today.

Sitting down with "company,"
She puts her dolly on her knee,
Then fills each little cup with tea
In such a gracious way.

She charmingly begins to chat
About her husband, her new hat,
And then announces her stuffed cat
Had kittens yesterday.

So feminine, so worldly wise,
And as I watch I realize
The mother she is learning to be
Is being patterned after me.

Kay Andrew

$\mathcal{W}$hat is a daughter?
>As well to ask, "What is a sunrise?"
>Each girl-child born brings unique warmth
>and light into her special corner of the world.
>This is a beauty which must be seen,
>a joy which must be felt to be believed.

Edward Cunningham

The sweet memories of her childhood,
the joy and happiness of her love today,
the bright dreams for all her tomorrows —
these are the blessings of a daughter.

Mary Ann Lowden

This Is a Daughter

A daughter is one of life's dearest gifts —
    a blessing from above ...
She's laughter, warmth and feminine charm ...
    she's thoughtfulness and love.
A daughter brings a special joy
    that comes from deep inside,
And as she grows to womanhood
    she fills your heart with pride.
The love she gives so freely
    is a rare and beautiful gift ...
She brings the sunshine right indoors
    and gives your heart a lift.
With every busy, happy year
    she's dearer than before ...
Through every stage ... through every age ...
    you love her even more.

George Webster Douglas

Set in Gill Sans, a typeface designed for
Monotype Corporation by British sculptor-
engraver-typographer Arthur Gill.

Book design by Leanne Mishler.